8 Emerald Hill Road is one of the first areas of Singapore where former dwellings of Peranakans - Chinese/Malay settlers converted to Christianity - have been restored to their original architectural forms.

9 This general view highlights building developments in the commercial core of this huge Asian metropolis: in the foreground are the typical two-storey buildings with porticos occupied by offices, stores and craftmen's workshops; towering behind them are the high-rise headquarters of the world's leading multinationals.

10-11 Dark has descended on the "Emporium of the South Seas" - as Singapore used to be known in the days when it was a British colony - but lights still shine out from the skyscraper offices where workaholic Singaporeans labour on well into the night.

known for sure is that the city eventually developed into a flourishing centre of trade.The first documentary proof of its existence dates back to the 13th century: by this time it had gained sufficient importance to attract the attention of great Oriental powers, including the Cola rulers of India, emperors of Thailand and kings of Java. Countless struggles by foreign states determined to gain possession of the city and oust this or that governor who held sway over the island proved ineffectual. Eventually other settlements and ports were established on other shores, to meet the needs of growing trade. And the once flourishing Singha Pura started a period of slow decline: its name gradually disappeared from maps and from the annals of history, and was eventually swallowed up by oblivion and the jungle. One of the last eye-witness accounts of the ancient City of the Lion was provided in 1330 by Wang Ta-Yuan, a Chinese writer and traveller: he described the island's inhabitants as a band of pirates whose only activity, besides plundering the few vessels that passed close to its shores, was fishing. Centuries passed before Singapore emerged from its 'dark age', to a new future and a new image. On January 29, 1819, Sir Thomas Stamford Bingley Raffles, a young official serving with the British East India Company, came ashore on the island: undeterred by its far-from-hospitable terrain - a maze of swamps and jungle - he recognized it as a potential site for a free trade settlement on the route between China and India. And this is precisely what it became.From that day on Singapore never looked back: its economic power steadily developed and its urban territory expanded apace. And like all

flourishing cities, it began to attract people in search of fortune and prosperity. Chinese immigrants (repudiated by their Emperor or slaves of coolie-brokers) were the first to settle in this "new land", in 1821: Hoklo from Amoy, nomadic Hakka from the far north, Kheh from the south, Cantonese, Teochew, Hainanese, Kwongsai and Holchiu. Junks carrying hordes of men who owned nothing but the shirts on their backs came sailing over the China Sea to Singapore. The terrible famines that struck 19th century China were the primary cause of migration on such a vast scale. But the tragedy of the Chinese became the fortune of Singapore: in their dire poverty these men saw hard work as their only hope of securing a better future.The ethnic mélange of this "promised land" was assured by an influx that included Indians from the coasts of Malabar and Coromandel, Malays from closer shores, Arabs who came as merchants and then settled here, Portughese and Dutch during the colonial era, Javanese, Bugis - natives of present-day Celebes - and, more recently, Jews, Armenians, Europeans, as well as North-Americans and Australians in the last few decades. Many, perhaps too many, races and cultures were united under a single flag too rapidly to allow harmonious fusion of lifestyles, customs and traditions. But instead of the tensions or bitter rivalries that might be expected with such a racial mix, Singaporeans have found a successful formula for peaceful co-existence within a single 'ethnically-challenged' nation. Present-day Singapore is not a melting pot of races; it is a mosaic of innumerable pieces that have each conserved their own distinctive colour and identity and yet form a single, precious whole. On a land

area of 640 square kilometres, the size of the island, the city-state has a population of 2,800,000 which is 76% Chinese (but natives of different parts of China, and of different cultures), 15% Malay, 6.5% Indian and 2.5% Eurasian. These figures need be no cause for alarm. Harmony reigns here and not only because - as has been unkindly claimed - Singaporeans are all tuned to the same wavelength, i.e. the profit motive. To obtain a real insight into this complex world - which is both ancient and ultra-modern, different and multi-facetted - take a stroll around the city's residential districts and let your impressions and instincts lead the way. Awaiting the attentive traveller, someone who is looking for more than rock-bottom bargain prices or useless curios, is a journey across the entire continent of Asia, and many surprises. And what better way to move around the Oriental universe of Singapore than by trishaw? Admittedly it has a touristy air but there is no more effective way to get instantly in tune with your surroundings. Ready and waiting is your "driver", doubtless lean-bodied, short of breath, with a tired, wrinkled face that tells of a lifetime of hardship. He knows every backstreet of Chinatown, not just the places where thronging tourists go looking for perfectly pirated replicas of designer products; he knows every secret of the narrow lanes of Little India; he can take you to the very heart of the mosaic. Better still, hunt out one of these "open carriages" in the evening, when bright neon lights make the shopping centres of Orchard Road even more dazzling, and the contrast with the tiny little buildings of Chinatown is even more evident. After dark a different spirit seems to animate the Chinese quarter of Singapore: the air

buzzes with the sounds of teeming markets where you can buy delicious tropical fruit of mind-boggling shapes; small, impromptu bazaars with an anachronistic air spring up before your eyes; tiny, fast-walking figures of seemingly ageless Chinese women silently pass by; pale lights glint from half-shut doors; cages on sidewalks reveal unexpected pythons... Gazing upwards, you become aware of the façades of grand, colonial-style villas: by day they come to life with colourful silks, kites, fluttering flags, red-painted bird-cages; at night their blinds are closed, concealing customs and rites that have remained unchanged for centuries. Suddenly, as you turn into a darker street, your dream of ancestral China is interrupted: seemingly out of context as it rises before you is a pyramid-shaped structure, a multitudinous assembly of variously coloured statues that have little in common with the almond eyes and other unmistakable features of the Chinese. The building is in fact an Indian temple; at night it appears to doze, by day the Sri Mariamman Hindu Temple comes alive with vibrant colours, rustling silk sarees and scattered flowers, part and parcel of the rituals performed in this place of worship. But the dream must now end. To take you back to the reality of modern Singapore, with its towering skyscrapers and tree-lined avenues, the trishaw must join the traffic on a main city thoroughfare. Here cars go speeding past, indifferent to their fellow road users: the frenzied pace of Singapore life is all too plain to see. Your fanciful journey fades from view but one certainty remains: it is in the city streets that the real mystery - the secret of Singapore's power and success - is revealed to those who go in search of it.

16 Pictured here are two pieces of France, transplanted to Singapore: the photo above is of the embassy, the one below shows the ambassador's residence. Set in beautifully tended gardens amid luxuriant vegetation, these snowy-white buildings are in classic colonial style: there are many fine examples of this type of architecture in the city's smartest neighbourhoods.

16-17 Urban development schemes may have rapidly turned the city into a 20th century metropolis but earlier buildings have survived. Almost the entire population has left the traditional native dwellings to be re-housed in apartment buildings from 10 to 20 storeys high, erected at an amazing rate (in the boom years, one apartment every 17 minutes); however, handsome old homes of the colonial era - the photo is of Alkaff Mansion - still punctuate the greener areas of the city.

20 The modern face of Singapore greets you at practically every turn. This sculpture by Salvador Dali' is in the OUB Plaza, near Raffles Place.

21 The forward-looking spirit of modern Singapore is very effectively symbolized by this fountain of bold, sinuous design, in chromed steel. On the left, the Merlion (a symbol of the city state of Singapore) stands guard at the mouth of the Singapore River.

23 The very latest electronic gadgets, the most recent miracles of advanced technology, top designer names, fabulous jewellery: all this, and more besides, can be bought in Orchard Road. Each shopping mall tries to outdo its neighbours with ever more impressive architecture, original decorations, eye-catching window displays and amazing offers, all designed to pull in crowds of shoppers who, once
over the threshold, will find it hard to resist the arrays of tempting goods on show. Orchard Road is indeed a shopper's paradise.

24 Guests at big hotels, like the Westin
Plaza on the left, almost always have
opportunities to soak up the tropical
sunshine within a stone's throw of the city.

25 The multiethnic face of Singapore is seen in Orchard Road, where thronging shoppers include locals as well as tourists. The rapid cultural and economic growth of the city owes much to the presence and co-existence of numerous different ethnic groups.

26-27 Tiny two-storey houses form a long terrace overlooking the Singapore River; until twenty or thirty years ago dwellings of this kind covered the entire area. A comparison with the skyscrapers of the business district gives an immediate idea of the forceful wind of change that has swept across the city. But even in this broad-spanning process of modernization and innovation, due regard has always been paid to the traditions and cultural heritage of the people of Singapore.

30 The first rays of the sun cast their warm colours onto the façade of the Empress Place building and neighbouring buildings, while the reflections in the still waters of the Singapore River produce a series of striking chromatic effects.

31 Night has now descended on the city: on the left of the picture is the Duxton Hotel, built in the heart of Tanjung Pagar admist rows of pubs, restaurants and quaint shops in one of Singapore's major conservation area.

*T*here are people who regard the City of the Lion as a kind of Oriental Disneyland, a place where order reigns and nothing - whether it be pure entertainment or the realities of everyday life - is left to chance. These individuals lack the humility needed to analyze and understand, rather than simply judge: they have not succeeded in delving down to the roots of this city-state and grasping the full significance of its plethora of cultures and traditions. Since independence in 1959 development policy has - it's true - been based almost entirely on three cornerstone principles: law and order, cleanliness and capitalism. But Singapore's enormous versatility and its success in integrating huge ethnic groups (without sacrificing the distinctive identity of each) has enabled it to test its strength against the rest of the world - and win. In worldwide ratings the city has achieved outstanding positions, for instance per capita earnings second only, in Asia, to Japan. Singapore is now unstoppable: it is heading towards an economic and technological future that many other nations will envy. And what better symbol of this future than the towering skyscrapers which fringe the Singapore River and are now shooting up in every part of the city? And yet the city-planners' approach to urban development is indicative of the modern spirit of Singapore, which aims to become a "tropical city of excellence" (as one of its most recent institutional advertising campaigns declares): the old districts with their dilapidated two-storey houses are not being bulldozed to make room for new buildings with more space; on the contrary, to safeguard the identity of the nation, they are being restructured as

testimonials to Singapore's past (in some cases still fairly recent). This does not stop the steel and glass giants from relentlessly racing heavenwards, each vying to be seen as the most formidable expression of power. The most recent projection of this urban model is the Singapore International Convention and Exhibition Center, a huge facility containing offices, shopping centres, hotels, congress centres, exhibition halls and much more. Its construction involved not only urban development, economic and financial studies: great importance was also attributed to 'Feng-shui', the Chinese art of geomancing, based on the interactivity of wind and water and considered an essential means of designing buildings harmonious with the laws of the universe. Singaporeans' regard for this 'pseudo-science' is significantly revealing. But Singapore is essentially a place where figures speak loudest of all, where business is business. It is a hot spot of the computer industry, the Silicon Valley of the Equator. It is a major centre of world business and trade. No fewer than 159 international banks have offices here; after all, as a hub of banking and finance, Singapore is third in the world, after London and New York. It is therefore hardly surprising that over 11,000 people - businessmen and tourists - arrive in this city-state every day. When it comes to figures on daily traffic, Singapore takes some beating. Consider the port, for example: at one time it depended for custom on adventurers seeking their fortune in the China Sea, the kind of characters who populate the novels of Joseph Conrad; today it is the busiest port in the world, and a major transshipment point for raw materials exported by nearby states like Thailand,

32 With its nighttime colours the city is transformed: streets and squares look totally different in the light shining from windows and street lamps, as well as the more colourful lights of restaurants, bars and night spots. Visible in the photo above are the characteristic red Chinese lanterns that add a festive air to Scotts, on the street of the same name; below is a café, on Orchard Road. The favourable climate means that, for much of the year, Singapore's nightlife can be enjoyed out of doors.

32-33 Another popular place with many restaurants and clubs is Boat Quay, right on the waterfront of the Singapore River. The typically Chinese vessel in the foreground adds a characteristic and unique touch to the scene.

34 The plans for Singapore's
redevelopment and improvement did not
destroy all evidence of the previous
vernacular architecture: the old two-storey
houses along Boat Quay were not
demolished and replaced by functional
modern buildings but instead totally
renovated. The outcome is an unusual but
undeniably attractive combination of
harmonious lines and vibrant colours.

35 In the Emerald Hill district, the homes
of Peranakans have also been carefully
restored. Little has changed in these
streets in the space of a century.

36 Alkaff Mansion was once a private home; now this elegant colonial-style building provides a fitting backdrop for a very fine restaurant where skilled chefs prepare the most typical specialities of Malaysian/Indonesian cuisine such as rijsttafel.

36-37 One of the focal points of city development schemes has been the renovation and refurbishment of the large, white colonial villas, situated mostly in the hilly parts of the city. This picture shows the more or less omnipresent features of these small-scale architectural gems: two-floor structure, garden with lush vegetation and inviting pool.

38-39 and 39 bottom Seen here are some interiors of Peranakan houses along Emerald Hill Road. The décor and furnishings point to an eclectic amalgam of styles but with nonetheless stunning results.

39 top The front doors of private dwellings open onto the porticos along Blair Road, further evidence of the predominating influence of the Chinese way of life.

42 Flags flutter in the wind on the arched bridge leading to the gateway of the Chinese Garden. The style of architecture most prominent here brings to mind the Summer Palace in Beijing, and particularly the buildings of the Sung dynasty. The park covers an area of over 13 hectares and contains all the features typical of Chinese garden tradition, from arched red bridges to handsome pavilions.

43 A towering presence in the Chinese Garden is an elegant Chinese pagoda, standing seven floors high; surrounding it are magnificent trees and manicured lawns.

Malaysia and Indonesia. The port has the facilities to handle over 800 vessels at any time of day and in any period of the year. It goes without saying that the pace of work is frenetic. A 40 ton container is loaded or unloaded every 15 seconds, a truly amazing record. Just about every kind of commodity and merchandise is processed and traded here (including tin, jute, rubber, coffee, rice, timber and spices). Crude oil is refined here too: in terms of volumes handled, Singapore's refineries occupy third place worldwide.

Singapore's outstanding track record as an ultra-efficient port has been achieved thanks to automated control of cargo handling operations. And yet only a short distance beyond the Strait of Malacca, this model organization structure, entirely computer-controlled, is something other nations can only dream of; in the ports of Indonesia goods are still unloaded by hand and ships have changed little from the vessels that docked here centuries ago. By concentrating its resources on information technology, Singapore has played the winning card. The city runs smoothly thanks to artificial intelligence. What started as an experiment is now problem-free reality. The National Computer Board has, for example, introduced a unique passport control system: foreigners' documents are checked in as little as 30 seconds, Singaporeans' in half that time. City traffic - traffic-lights included - is controlled by a sensor-based electronic system able to optimize flow in real time, a truly outstanding achievement. Even the construction industry is feeling the influence of electronics: Singapore is being slowly transformed into the networked metropolis of the future, right from its very

foundations. What more is there to say about this forward-looking city-state? No description of Singapore would be complete without mention of its glorious colonial past, a legacy present not only in its urban layout and buildings but in the city's ambition-driven spirit, vowed to conquest and victory. If you trace the footsteps of Sir Thomas Raffles you will breathe in the air of old England, on an island only a matter of miles from the Equator. Still fronting the slow-moving waters of the Singapore River - although now overshadowed by concrete and steel towers - are the gracious buildings erected in the days of the British Empire: the typically colonial, white structures that house the Parliament, the City Hall, the Empress Place building, the Victoria Theatre and Memorial Hall. On the hills too are examples of British colonial architecture: huge mansions encircled by the emerald-green vegetation of the tropics still occupy their enviable sites, surrounded by jungle while commanding fine views of the city. Singaporeans show great love and respect for nature. Not only is it the "ultimate of all things" according to Tao doctrine; it is an omnipresent part of their everyday lives, which is why the city's many parks and gardens - the Bird Park, the Chinese gardens, the Japanese gardens - are greatly admired and tended with the utmost care. It is far from easy to reveal, with mere words, the underlying spirit of this island, situated on the southernmost point of the Malay Peninsula where the Indian Ocean meets the Pacific, gateway to Malaysia and Indonesia, at the crossroads separating Indian Asia from Chinese Asia. It is perhaps simplest to take Singapore at face value, admiring it for what it is and stands for.

46 Many of the major events organized in Singapore take place along the banks of the Singapore River. The Hong Bao Special festivities are held in January and February: members of Chinese communities all over the world come to exhibit and buy the most typical products of their traditional culture.

47 The Wisma Atria Shopping Centre, in the picture, puts its opulence on display. At a first, superficial glance it may seem hard to distinguish between all these glitzy shopping centres. But each one has been designed to look unique and unmistakable to the thousands of visitors who pack Orchard Road all year long.

48 The UOB Plaza at the centre of this picture is the tallest skyscraper in Singapore: at the very top is a revolving restaurant from which diners can enjoy stunning views over the city.

50 Sentosa Island is just off the southern shore of Singapore and linked by the Sentosa Causeway. There are also other more original ways of crossing: on a characteristic ferry boat or - rather more unusual - by cable car. This small island is a major recreational facility offering assorted amusements: white-sand beaches fringed with tropical palms, musical fountains, the Asean village with reconstructions of traditional houses, gardens, museums and Undersea World where over 2,000 different species of sea creatures living in a gigantic acquarium can be observed from a 100-metre transparent underwater tunnel.

51 This aerial view of Sentosa shows the south beach and Shangri-La's luxurious Rasa Sentosa Resort situated on the southwest tip of the island. Visible in the background are the countless ships that sail from Singapore's port - in terms of goods handled, the world's largest - to all four corners of the world.

52-53 Singapore - with South Korea, Hong Kong and Taiwan - is one of the four dragons of South-east Asia. Never is its cityscape monotonous: by day - and by night - unpredictable, shifting light seems to transform the smooth surfaces of its buildings, creating an illusion of continuous change.

54-55 Like the many other shopping centres on Orchard Road, the front of Lucky Plaza is always decked out to attract shoppers; as Christmas approaches, the decorations become even brighter and more festive.

55 Along Orchard Road an attractive young Chinese girl smiles at the camera.

58 Also inside these ultra-modern shopping malls - shrines to consumerism at its most rampant - a spending-inducive ambience is subtly created with decorative effects and cleverly designed lighting systems: this photograph shows the atrium of Wisma Atria Shopping Centre, another huge shopping centre on Orchard Road.

59 Not only is there an unbelievable assortment of merchandise on show in Orchard Road: the very image of the city is presented to the scrutiny of an international public. Highlighted in this photo are the innovative and imposing structures of the Paragon shopping centre, another place where shoppers can buy anything and everything.

60-61 As well as the hi-tech architecture almost emblematic of Orchard Road, there are places like Orchard Point: here, in a return to tradition, green roofs typical of Chinese buildings are used together with red Chinese lanterns donned to celebrate the Chinese New Year.

61 Light comes cascading down the façades of the shopping malls during the pre-Christmas period, transforming Orchard Road into a small-scale Oriental Las Vegas.

62-63 The most recent urbanization schemes implemented in the city have made specific provision for districts where Singaporeans and tourists can spend their leisure. Entire blocks, for instance, are now occupied by restaurants, cafés and bars. The city's eating places offer every imaginable gourmet delight of Chinese, Indian and Malay cuisines, as well as many others. Pictured on the left are the crowded tables of Clarke Quay; in the centre, a few of the East Coast restaurants, where fish is a speciality; on the right, New Bugis Street, where eating places offer a wide choice of exciting menus at very affordable prices.

64 Singapore has a population of about 3 million, made up of many ethnic groups: each one preserves and hands down its own culture, religion and traditions. Despite this diversity of race and creed - Chinese, Malays, Indians, Pakistanis, Armenians, Arabs, Europeans, Jews - racial tension has rarely been a major problem here and the inhabitants of this city-state live amicably side by side. The photo shows a trader selling baskets and goods woven from raffia and straw, outside his shop in Arab Street.

65 The normally elegant hairstyles of young Malay women are given a more ornamental look for Hari Raya, the festivities celebrating the Muslim New Year.

66-67 The Indian community accounts for about 7 percent of Singapore's population and many of its members live in a quarter called Little India, along Serangoon Road. Time-honoured traditions and customs are maintained and handed down to new generations: even all the age-old rituals of wedding ceremonies are observed, down to the smallest detail.

67 A young Indian woman dressed in richly decorated garments prepares to dance in the Chingay Parade, an annual event celebrating the Chinese New Year in which the various ethnic communities in Singapore often take part.

68 This young Chinese woman is lighting a votive candle. Numerous places of worship have sprung up in Singapore, thanks also to the peaceful and tolerant co-existence of the city's many different communities.

69 Burning joss sticks is a ceremonial rite during prayer, to which Buddhists attribute great importance: the scene depicted here is taken in the Thian Hock Keng temple one of the oldest Chinese temples in Singapore.

70 The worn expression on the face of this old trishaw driver says a lot about the physical effort demanded by this old and traditional means of earning a living, now gradually disappearing.

71 The trishaw has long been established as a means of transport in Singapore. Originally there was the rikshaw, a two-wheeled passenger vehicle drawn by a man on the trot; after World War II, when bicycles became common, a sidecar was added to the two wheels: this atypical taxi was still driven by a man, but required considerably less effort. Cars have now taken over from this original form of transport: only 200 of the city's original 'fleet' of 9,000 trishaws now remain, and they are used solely by tourists.

72 When celebrations are in progress for
the Chinese New Year, which falls in
January/February, Chinatown becomes a
funfair of colour and light. Rows of make-
shift stalls lined the streets peddling typical
items that tradition demands: incense
flowers, decorations, barbecued meats,
greeting cards and many other New Year
delicacies.

73 All day long, and late into the night too, the narrow streets of Chinatown are packed with fascinated tourists and native Singaporeans in search of the best festive buys and decorations. During the Chinese New Year, Singapore - and Chinatown in particular - takes on a different look. The city's usual spectrum of colours succumbs to the fiery shades of red, which predominates in all the decorations; in the temples dozens and dozens of joss sticks are lit as an offering to the deities. The celebrations last for 15 days, ending normally with a spectacular display of fireworks.

76-77 The religious and secular festivals respected and celebrated in Singapore are many, and span the whole year. These two pictures were taken during the famous "Festival of the Hungry Ghosts".

79 The offerings neatly arranged on huge tables for the Festival of the Hungry Ghosts do not stop at food alone. As these pictures show, the gifts can include paper figurines, incense, even money...

80 The long tables spread with offerings
for the spirits are prepared with great
care: the banquet is mounted in areas
where street markets are held, and
endless time is spend installing elaborate
decorations and preparing tasty things to
eat.

*81 Some priests are eating the spirits'
"leftovers". According to traditional ritual,
no food must be wasted although it is said
that, once the ghosts have partaken of the
feast, all the remaining food mysteriously
becomes quite tasteless.*

82 and 83 right The scenes depicted here are from the procession to mark Thaipusam, celebrated by Singapore's Hindu community in January/February. The rituals performed by devotees involve presenting offerings and asking pardon from the god Subramanya.

83 left After fasting and praying for three weeks, the devotees are almost in a state of trance as they prepare for the procession, donning bright yellow garments and ornaments. To atone for their sins or to seek divine favours they walk the whole way barefoot or wearing spiked sandals and they pierce their bodies with spikes or hooks and their cheeks and tongue with long silver pins

and needles (top photo). To further appease the deities, the penitents carry "kavadi", richly adorned metal arches which can weigh over 30 kilos (bottom photo). The procession ends at the Chettiar Temple in Tank Road; the Hindu devotees arrive there in a state of total collapse and, once relieved of the heavy "kavadi", are restored in full – pierced skin and wounds are magically healed.

84 During the Lantern Festival the Chinese Garden explodes with light and colour. Pictured in this photo is a small temple - similar in style to the Summer Palace in Beijing - overlooking a pond decorated with carp-shaped paper lanterns.

85 Shining through the dark of the Chinese Garden are countless paper lanterns with a multitude of shapes and decorative patterns.

86-87 Seen here in close-up, the lanterns give off a warm light which brightens the night air in the Chinese Garden. Situated at Jurong, in the far west of the island, the garden covers an area of almost 14 hectares. This part of Singapore has undergone rapid development, with a continuous influx of modern manufacturing facilities and new businesses. But the area set aside for the gardens remains intact and is carefully conserved.

88-89 *These scenes are from a performance of Chinese opera or "wayang", an art form that brings secular traditions of the past back to life, on stage: performers devote years to study and training and the make-up and ornate costumes also demand exceptional skills and long experience.*

90-91 Haw Par Villa, (fondly remembered as the original Tiger Balm Gardens) along the Pasir Panjang Road, offers a man-made paradise for tourists: there are many statues depicting stories of Chinese mythology, dragon rides, acrobats and all sorts of attractions to entertain children and anyone else wanting to spend a few carefree hours.

92 National Day is August 9, the date when, in 1965, Singapore became an independent republic. The anniversary is commemorated each year with plenty of flags, colour and general high spirits.

93 This photograph shows Singapore's national stadium during a colourful and spectacular display staged to mark the SEA Games (Southeast Asian Games) . Sport plays an important part in the everyday life of Singaporeans: being keen athletes, they play soccer, golf, tennis, squash and water sports to name a few.

94-95 The skyscrapers of Singapore are wrapped in the warm light of the setting sun. But even approaching night does not attenuate the breakneck pace of life in the city: only the focus of attention changes, from daytime work to nighttime pleasures.

96 With gaily coloured paper fish floating in the ponds and countless red lanterns the Lantern Festival adds a new note of light and colour to the attractive setting of the Chinese Garden.